A long time ago, some dinosaurs lived in a forest on the side of a big volcano.

They had leaves to eat, and water to drink. The volcano stayed asleep, and life was good.

But one day, the volcano started to shake. It roared and it rumbled. Black smoke shot out from its top.

Red-hot rocks flew into the air. The big, slow dinosaurs could not get out of the way. Some of them were hit by the flying rocks.

Then rivers of red-hot rock came down the side of the volcano.
<u>Lava!</u>
The red-hot lava set fire to the trees.

Soon all the forest was on fire, and black smoke filled the air.

Most of the dinosaurs did not get away in time.Some died in the smoke, and some died in the fires.

But four big dinosaurs did get away.

They ran downhill until they came to a lake. They went into the water and they kept on going.

When the water became deeper in the middle of the lake, they kicked at the bottom with their strong legs, and began to swim.

They walked and swam, and swam and walked, all the way across the lake.

Their long necks kept their heads
up out of the water, all night long.

In the morning, they climbed out of the lake. Now they were a long way from the volcano, and the red-hot lava, and the fire and the smoke.

They saw green trees all around them.
They had leaves to eat, and water to
drink, and life was good again.